ICE CREAM

POETRY IN MANY FLAVORS

ERIC LAWRENCE FRAZIER MBA

THE POWER IS NOW MEDIA, INC.
RADIO I TV I MAGAZINE I SEMINARS

CONTENTS

ICE CREAM
Poetry in Many Flavors
By
Eric Lawrence Frazier MBA

***

Thank you for taking the time to order and support my very first poetry collection. I just have one more request. If you could head over to Amazon and leave a 5-star review.

Reviews are the lifeline for any author and this will help other readers find and enjoy my book.

Best,

Eric L. Frazier

SCAN ME

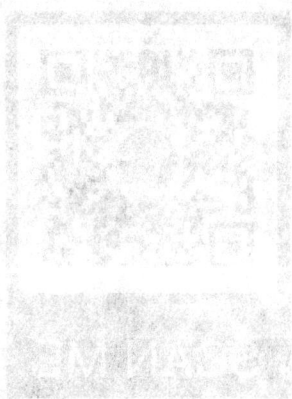

ERIC LAWRENCE FRAZIER, MBA POETRY BOOKS

COPYRIGHT

ICE CREAM
Poetry in Many Flavors

Copyright © 2025
The Power Is Now Media
Volume 1

www.ThePowerIsNow.com
@ThePowerisnow

ISBN 13: 978-1-949722-03-1 (ebook)
ISBN13: 9781949722031 (paperback)
ISBN 13: 978-1-949722-00-0 (hardcover)

ACKNOWLEDGMENTS

First, I would like to thank God and the inspiration that He provides me to write. I love the Love of God and I am humbled to be saved by his grace and mercy. This book is dedicated to all who know Him and to those who are still searching. May you find Him. I want to thank my beautiful wife Ruby of 39 years. I love you more than words can say. You have been my rock and my greatest cheerleader from the day we first met. There is not a day that goes by that I am not grateful for all you have done and continue to do for our family and me. I can't imagine life without you. Thank you to my for wonderful daughters Jessica, Briana, Erica and Raela. Each one of you holds a special place in my heart. You are powerful, beautiful and highly intelligent women who are doing great things in life. I am very proud of all of you. To my grandchildren Carrah, Chloe and Cameron I love you very much and cannot wait to see the impact you have on the world. To Virgil and Jordan, you are men of God and of valor. I am thankful for the love you have for Briana and Raela and the life you are making together. I love you both and I am proud to be your father-in-law and for the blessing you are to my family. You all inspire me by the very different lives you're living and great things you are accomplishing. I am very proud to be the Patriarch of the family and I love you all very much.

Thank you, Kim Collier, Director of The Power Is Now Publishing. Your daily support, reminders, and expertise in publishing this book have been extremely valuable. I started with a vision and now we are publishing several books. Thank you for staying on me and working with me through the entire process. This book would not have happened without you. Thank you Goldy Ponce, Graphic designer and leader of The Power Is Now Graphic Design team, your amazing eye for design coupled with your ability to implement exactly what I need has resulted in an amazing cover that captures the true essence of this book. To Val Salomaki and Sheila Gilmore, both leaders of our Technology and Marketing team, you are awesome! It is because of your daily support, great work and professionalism that this book and others will receive the attention they deserve. I appreciate your work very much.

To those of you who are reading this book right now, thank you for taking a chance on me, and the time out of your busy life, to read my poetry. I hope you enjoy the book and share it with others.

DEDICATION

To my loving wife of 39 years, Ruby.
Thank you for your support and inspiration in every aspect of life. To my
brothers and sister whom I love very much and my spiritual family of
believers and leaders whose love for God and for me keeps my faith strong. I
love you all more than ice cream.

PREFACE

This is my first book of poetry, and I pray that you will enjoy reading it as much as I enjoyed writing it. The poems represent almost twenty years of my life, and there is more to come.

What is poetry to me? It is a personal expression of my feelings and ideas about everything and everyone in my life. No one can escape my poetry. This can be a good thing or a bad thing, depending on who you are. So be careful you may find yourself in one of my poems.

I cannot sit down and just write poetry. I have to be moved to write it, and that often happens at the most inconvenient times. It comes to me early in the morning or sometimes in the afternoon or sometimes very late in the evening. I can go weeks, months, or even years without feeling the need to write what I'm feeling, believing, seeking, or concerned about. Something has to move me. It could be the sound of children playing or the sound of someone's voice. It could be a commercial on television or a news event about a disaster somewhere in the world. It could be an argument with my wife which I never win, or a disappointment caused by myself or others. It just has to be something. Something meaningful, something substantive, something eventful has to arrest my attention for a moment and move me to write.

To me the best thing about writing poetry is the experience and process. It is the excitement that comes over me when I am moved to write and the words begin to flow through my mind faster than I can write them down or type them. It is the emotions that run through my body and the feeling of excitement as I near the end of writing the poem.

It is very intimate and spiritual. It is also emotional and draining. Sometimes the process and experience is so intense that I begin to ask myself questions like, "Where did that come from?" or make statements like "I can't believe I wrote that!" It's a truly ethereal experience.

The irony of writing poetry for me is that finishing the poem is somewhat anticlimactic because I really don't want the process to end. I just want the words or thoughts to continue to flow. But when it ends, it truly ends and what a letdown it is until I am moved to write again. I find myself going to bed hoping to be awakened by a dream or flash of thought that forces me to grab my pen and paper and begin to write and throw myself into the process. Rarely does it happen these days probably because of the stress of running multiple businesses. Also, I am sure that getting older also has a lot to do with it. My memory and patience have both diminished significantly over time but I continue to write.

I hope that you find these poems interesting and that in reading them they transport you into another realm of thought as the witness and observer of your life circumstances, your mind and its random thoughts and the impermanence of your existence, as you can sense it, in the universe. May God bless you and allow the poet in you take you to places that you have not been before in thought and presence.

~Eric Lawrence Frazier, Poet

PEACE

Looking for peace in this place?

Striving to make it in this rat race?

Just pray that Jesus keeps you on pace

The earth is the devil's headquarters

His throne room and home base

Don't look for peace in this place.

If you want true peace,

find it in God.

In the outside world peace is just a façade.

I often throw fits

Even wonder if I am losing my wits

Seeking peace in the Devil's pit.

Deep down I know it doesn't exist.

The pursuit of peace here can make you sick.

The peace in the world is all a façade

It doesn't mean anything if you do not have God.

If you want peace, do not look for it here.

In this world, there is nothing but fear,

It's like living under clouds that never clear.

Or sensing a terrible feeling that the end is near.

If you want true peace, find it in God,

In the outside world, peace is just a façade.

The world would have you believe that peace here is possible,

But I'm here to tell you that peace can only be found in the gospel.

Peace from a troubled home life,

Peace from living a thug life,

Peace from alcoholism and drug addiction

Peace from depression and bad obsession

Peace from the loss of innocence, and inordinate affections

Peace from strife and bad intentions,

Real peace with God without human inventions.

. . .

There will always be the naive, who are easily deceived

Into thinking the world can give them what they need.

If you think you do not need the peace of God,

Then you are truly caught up in the world's façade.

Have peace right now, between you and God,

And don't get caught up in this world's façade.

RAELA

Just four feet tall yet she thinks she is bigger than them all.
Her sisters, that is, who try to keep her small,

And out of their conversations
When their friends call.

Raela is six going on twenty-six
And makes all of her older sister's sick
Too grown for her own good.

It's like she grew up straight out of the hood
Dancing and singing rap songs
As if she really knew the words and understood

About blackness, relationships

shooting and worse.

When I look at her,

I wonder where she came from:

Lighter skinned than all of us,

And always wanting to have fun,

Totally outgoing and fears no one.

Quick to fight any of her three sisters

And run to tell her mother or me what they have done.

Raela is bright and so full of energy.

If she were a nuclear reactor, she could run a city.

Always moving and jumping around,

Can't keep still or stop making sounds.

She is so funny I just don't know what to do.

And so I just try to keep her active

And doing well in school.

She is all grown up now and about to get married.

Oh my God she is about to get married

Thank God it's not in a hurry.

. . .

Degree in one hand and engagement ring in the other.

She is going to live her best life and not for others.

Ruby we saved the best for last.

Don't get mad Big Sisters. We love you too.

IVERY SUMMER

Happy Birthday to Ivery who defies Father Time because she is Summer all the time and gets better every year like the most expensive wines.

Happy Birthday to a lady whose style and sophistication sets high expectations for every woman of her time.

Happy Birthday to a sister who is down to earth

And loves to keep it real.

Ivery will give you the clothes off her back,

Take you home, and feed you a meal.

Happy Birthday to a child of God

Who lives out her love for God every day.

The love of God is in her eyes, her demeanor,

Her ability to listen and to relate.

Ivery has been through and out

Under and over many storms in her life

But God has been faithful.

So on this birthday,

When the celebration comes to an end,

In the stillness of the night,

When you think of your plight and

How God continues to keep you in the fight,

Be thankful that

He is the way, the truth, and the light.

He will always give you the path to what is right and

He has blessed you with spiritual sight to see His path for you in spite of the night, but darkness cannot prevail in the light.

Hallelujah!

Weeping May endureth for a night

But joy cometh in the morning.

Happy Birthday, Ivery!

Sing a song of gladness and rejoice in the Lord always,

Because He has and always will have your back.

RUBY

I'm sitting *on* the whitewashed wicker furniture,
　　Looking across the room at sleeping beauty.
The ceiling fan is buzzing with noise
And blowing a breeze cool enough to make you sleepy.

The television is showing a black and white movie
So luminous it hurts your eyes.
Yet sleeping beauty, unaware of her surroundings,
Has snuggled in the pink flowered pillows
That cover the couch and has sprawled her long
Lanky legs and slender body the full length of it.

Her head is propped up by her hand and shoulder.

The other hand firmly placed between her thighs

To capture the heat generated by her body.

Her hair is laying wildly on her head,

Eyes closed and mouth slightly open.

Who is this woman whose beauty and grace rival

The Nubian queens of our great homeland in times past?

I feel as though I am standing on holy ground,

Blessed by her presence and beauty.

Moved by the simplicity and peacefulness of her slumber,

I restrain myself from waking her,

Feeling compelled to blanket her with my affection.

Would she respond and send me to a realm of

Ecstasy unknown by a mere mortal like me?

Or does she belong to another?

Perhaps a god or an angel in heaven,

Or maybe she's just a transient apparition

Parading in my dream?

Suddenly, reality has slapped me in the face,

As I rise from the whitewashed wicker loveseat

Only to look down to a cluttered floor

And up to a messy countertop.

The children are asleep and so without making a peep

I closed the curtains, lock the door,

And thank God for a home,

A wife, children, and a life with Ruby.

ICE CREAM

I love you, ice cream.

You make me crazy and sick at the same time

Because I'm lactose intolerant.

I dream about you in my sleep.

I think about my favorite flavors all the time

And the special moments we have shared together.

In times of celebration

I can always count on rocky road to be the

Highlight of the evening.

When I'm out and about town and running errands,

I can always count on mint 'n chip at the local ice cream parlor

To give me that boost of energy I need.

In times of sadness and despair,

Feelings that I try to avoid,

Vanilla is my best friend and along with her partners,

Oatmeal and raisin cookie,

Together they provide me the comfort and solace I am looking for.

I love you ice cream and I will never leave you.

You are my friend,

And I thank you for the joy you continue to bring to my life.

I look forward to our next celebration

When all of my favorite flavors and friends can come together.

I miss strawberry, butter pecan, and black walnut.

Black walnut was my Dad's favorite ice cream.

He introduced me to black walnut

And we have been best friends ever since, although

we have not spoken in some time.

I am meeting with pecan praline tonight for dinner

And I am certain we are going to have a great time.

You see, ice cream allows you to think and speak.

It doesn't interrupt you or try to solve your problems.

It doesn't get impatient and rush you

To get to the point of what you have to say.

Ice cream just sits there and looks beautiful

And sweet and melts as it listens to you.

It doesn't judge you or get angry with you.

Ice cream just makes you feel good

By being present and sweet.

It doesn't leave a bad taste in your mouth.

It's sweet and not salty.

You look forward to your next time together.

Sometimes we need to stop whatever we are doing,

Find the nearest ice cream parlor,

Sit down, and relax in front of our

Favorite bowl of ice cream and focus

On the joy it brings us in the short

Time that it takes us to devour it.

Leave your worries at the office or house

And for a moment become a child again

And enjoy the simple happiness,

Albeit brief, that ice cream can bring.

In spite of the challenges we all have that seem to never end,

The disappointments we face from time to time,

The tragedy and sadness of life in the world,

It is good to know that ice cream will forever

Be a constant reminder that life can be very sweet.

You just need to grab a bowl, or a cup,

Or spoon, of ice cream and I promise

That in that moment, when you are fully present,

and the flavor has been introduced to your palate

You will find happiness.

I LOVE YOU MORE RUBY

I love you because I can't help myself.
I love you more than life itself.
I need you and I can't live without you.
Even though you make me crazy I love you.

When I think about how much I love you
I always come up short because I think I love you
More than whatever I come up with.

I love you more than this,
And I love you more than that
I love you more than all of what I can ever say
Because I love you more than words can say.

. . .

I love you more

Than symbols can represent,

Than sounds can make,

Than gestures can communicate,

Than art can portray,

Than emotions can feel,

Than eyes can see,

Than faces can change,

Than lips can curl,

Than minds can think,

Than arms can reach,

Than feet can run,

Than hearts can beat,

Than hair can grow,

Than noses can smell,

Than hands can touch,

Than eyelids can blink,

Than ears can hear,

Than tongues can taste,

Than stomachs can digest,

Than teeth can chew,

Than minds can dream,

Than bodies can sweat,

Than underarms can stink,

Than dirt on the earth,

Than all the grass on the dirt,

Than all the insects on the grass,

Than all the water on the earth,

Than all the fish in the water,

Than birds in the air,

Than animals that roam the earth,

Than sand on the beach,

Than vehicles on the road,

Than people who are dead.

What can I say?

I love you because I can't help myself.

I love you more than life itself.

I need you and I can't live without you.

Even though you make me crazy

I love you.

SIGHS

Sighs of trouble, sadness, or despair
Sounds the same as joy, peace-whispering air.

Sighs of passion, love, and hate
All sound the same but have different measures of pain.

Deep, deep, in the darkness of the mind
Lie sighs around just waiting for their time.

Straight from the chasm of grief and despair,
Or the windows of the soul when upon beauty
And love they behold.

Sighs, utterances that cannot be understood,

Cannot remain shut up within us when we love.

Trapped in the mind the sighs begin to moan,

The tongue groans, and the eyes begin to lie.

Sighs are deep from the soul,

Representing utterances that can't be told.

Affecting the mind, body, and soul after taking their toll,

Leaving us un-whole.

With love and emotions grown cold,

Our smiles turn to sadness,

No joy, just madness. Sighs.

BLACK BEAUTY

*H*igh yellow, brown sugar, dark plum,
Caramel, honeydew, mocha, walnut,
And vanilla crème are some of the
Many colors and distinctions of black beauty.

Long and short,
Curly and kinky,
Straight and flat hair
Are some of the many styles of black beauty.

Voluptuous, skinny,
Tall, short, big,
And small boned
Are some of the many figures and silhouettes of black beauty.

. . .

Large and petite chests,

Small and large behinds,

Full and small lips,

Wide and narrow hips,

Round and narrow faces,

High and low cheeks

Are some of the fabulous features of black beauty.

Long and short arms,

Large and small hands,

Big and tiny feet,

Long and short legs,

Are some of the fine instruments of black beauty.

There is beauty you see in the blackness of thee

That makes whatever God gave thee exciting to me.

When I see the black beauty in thee I am overwhelmed,

When I hear the voice of black beauty I am comforted,

When I feel the embrace of black beauty I am moved.

I hear and I'm amazed,

I feel and I'm amazed,

I see and I am wonderfully amazed.

Amazed at divine creativity

And thankful to be a beneficiary of black beauty.

I try to describe what I see and say lovely,

Beautiful, graceful, sultry, sexy, and pretty.

However, the limitation of language fails me miserably

To truly communicate what I see in black beauty.

I am silenced by my limited perception and vocabulary,

I am silenced by the reality that what

God has made is indescribable.

I am silenced and can only speak with my eyes

Because my tongue has lost its way.

The creator has outdone himself

And has molded dust into flesh

Which language could never describe

The Magnificence of black beauty.

If only I could shout from the mountain tops

The beauty I see.

As an admirer, and lover, of black beauty,

I say thank you, God,

For Your gift of black beauty to me.

Black beauty is the image of You

And cannot be described

By the ramblings of a mere mortal like me.

Nevertheless, black beauty gives me a glimpse of the essence of You,

The awesome beauty and love that must cover You.

Therefore, I love the beauty in black beauty,

Because I love the beauty of You.

I DON'T HAVE

✵

I don't have is the refrain of a song
We sing when we don't know what to do.

I don't have the money,
Not a single dime.

I don't have the when to spend,
Just no time.

I don't have the knowledge;
I didn't finish college.

I don't have the skill,
I am not good at making deals.

. . .

I don't have the resources,

Can't get help from my sources.

I don't have the courage

And don't want to be discouraged.

I don't have the motivation,

Inspiration, and truthfully the inclination.

I just have my song "I don't have"

That I sing when I don't know what to do.

I need a new song.

A song about victory and abundance.

A song about triumph over defeat.

A song about prosperity over poverty.

A song about hope and not despair.

A song about faith and not fear.

A song about confidence and assurance.

A song about what I can do and not what I can't do.

A song about what I have and not what I don't have.

I can sing that song,

I can sing it loud.

I can internalize that song; I can make that song my anthem.

I can sing, "I can do anything through Christ who strengthens me."

I can sing, "I can do anything through Christ who strengthens me."

That's my new song!

I will sing that song

When I am against incredible odds

I will sing that song

When I am faced with the opportunity to succeed.

I will sing that song

When faced with life's challenges.

I will sing that song

When fear comes into my mind,

I will sing that song

When doubt comes into my mind.

I will sing that song

When roadblocks are put in my way.

I will sing that song

When I don't have what I need.

I will sing that song

When I don't get cooperation from others.

I will sing that song

When I am denied access or opportunity.

I can do all things through Christ who strengthens me.

That's my song! I love that song!

It gives me strength when I am weak,

It gives me confidence when I need it.

It gives me the insight that God is in control of my life.

It gives me faith to know that He knows what I need even before I ask.

I got myself a new song.

I'm not singing that old song anymore.

How about you?

HAPPY BIRTHDAY RUBY

On this day that God has made

　　He brought you into this world as a little babe.

The world may not have been ready,

But I know you were my destiny.

I thank God for each year with you that

He has blessed me to be

And to see you grow older

And wiser is a gift to everybody.

You have grown to be a beautiful woman

Daughter, mother, and wife,

And God has blessed you to have faith in Jesus Christ

And enjoy the Christian life.

. . .

I know that this year of your life is just the beginning

Of more great things to come,

You have age on the run and he can't stop your fun.

Just keep on living, caring, blessing, singing,

Dreaming, learning, never being out-done.

I hope you live until Jesus comes.

I can't imagine life in this world without you,

It would be like the earth without the sun.

You are light, my number one,

You give me strength to carry on

And make my life so much fun.

I will love you until life in my body is done.

Happy Birthday.

HAPPY MOTHER'S DAY RUBY

*R*uby on this Mother's Day
I pray that God will give you a sense of pride
And accomplishment that you have never felt before.

You are the mother of four daughters,
A wonderful wife and so much more.

You are the foundation to our home,
Our comfort when we moan and groan,
Our support when we are away from home,
Our counselor when we know we are wrong.

You are the mother of four daughters,
A wonderful wife and so much more.

. . .

You are an intelligent,

Engaging conversationalist and never a bore.

You are thoughtful and considerate of others to the core,

You have style, beauty, and grace that no one can ignore.

You are the mother of four daughters,

A wonderful wife and so much more.

You are a strong Black woman

Who will never take less when there is more.

You are deep in the Word and spiritually you soar.

You always have a nurturing approach

And look to give others even more.

You are my wife,

My love who I will always adore,

Because you are the mother of four daughters,

A wonderful wife and so much more.

I love you and so much more.

NOW

Therefore, there is NOW no condemnation
For those who are in Christ Jesus, because through Christ Jesus the law of the
Spirit of life set me free from the law of sin and death.
(Roman 8: 1-2, NIV)

This gift of righteousness is present in us

And can never leave us,

Not now, tomorrow,

Next month or next year

Because now is the eternal reality to us

Who believe that Christ Jesus set us free

From sin, death, and mortality.

Now, not tomorrow

Because you had eight hours of sleep.

Tomorrow never comes

Even though you count the days of the week.

Now, not tomorrow

Because the sun will have risen and set.

The sun never stops shining on the earth,

So that's a losing bet.

Now, not because you count the days,

Weeks, months, and years,

A thousand years is like one day to the Lord

And the apostle Peter made that very clear.

Now is all you have.

Now you can be saved.

Right now!

Now, not tomorrow,

Not later today,

Not tonight, but now.

Not a dream, not a hope,

Not a wish to come true, but now.

Not a possibility,

Not a great idea to come, but now.

. . .

Now, not if you're good enough later, but now.

Not if you work hard enough later, but now.

Not if you worship long enough later, but now.

Not if you pray continually later, but now.

Not if you confess all your sins, but now.

Not if you acknowledge all your sins, but now.

Not if you think you have no sins, but now.

Not if you are no longer sinning, but now.

Not if you are not living in sin, but now.

Now, right now,

Right this hour,

This minute,

This second,

This very moment.

Now immediately,

Right here and now you must believe:

The gift of eternal life is free

Jesus' death, burial, and resurrection

Has set you free.

I BELIEVE IN ME

I believe in me.

Nappy hair, brown eyes and big lips,

I believe in me.

Big butt, short legs, and potbelly,

I believe in me.

Black skin, no ends, and major sins,

I believe in me.

Four eyes, nine lives, and talking jive,

I believe in me.

It's God, you see,

Who helps me to accept me?

To believe that I can be,

Whatever my mind chooses to be.

There is within me

A desire that God gave me.

To see what others cannot see,

To be what others dream to be,

To run as far as I can see,

To climb every mountain that stands before me,

To love my family and people close to me,

To love those who hate me,

To help others who come to me.

Why? Because I believe in me and

The power that lives in me.

He supports me to be all that I can be,

To strive in spite of what I see,

To live by faith that I can be

Whatever I want to be because

I believe in me.

HONEY DO'S

Honey do's, honey do's,
  My day is filled with honey do's.
Up in the morning at 6 o'clock
Sitting on the bed and taking stock.
Gotta do this and gotta do that,
If Ruby says one more thing
I'm going to crack.

Honey do's, honey do's,
My day is filled with honey do's.
Don't forget this and don't forget that,
Take out the trash and clean up the back.

Honey do's, honey do's,

My day is filled with honey do's.

Go get your haircut

And pick up my cleaning

And don't forget the groceries

We have been needing.

Honey do's, honey do's,

My day is filled with honey do's.

What's a man to do?

Go do your Honey do's!

THE LOVE OF A WIFE RUBY

When I think of the love of my wife a smile comes across my face

Because I'm happy to see her celebrate another birthday.

I wonder how my life would be without her.

Her love is sweeter than honey from a honeycomb.

I leave for work with anticipation of coming home

To spend time with my woman who is sweet to the bone.

I take in deeply the aroma of her love

And caress her skin that is smooth as a dove.

When my lips touch hers it's passionate, it's love!

I would climb the highest mountain or swim the deepest sea

To have just one moment of her love,

It's so precious to me.

. . .

I am so thankful that she is mine in matrimony

And to be the beneficiary of her love for eternity

Is truly God's gift to me.

It's amazing to be with someone

so endowed with beauty,

Love, and sensuality: she is my destiny.

God meant her for me.

I now know why. I love what I see

He placed His love in me

and gave her to me.

I should fall on my knees and praise Thee

for thou hast loved me And made me so happy

to be in love with a wife like thee,

Who gives of herself completely

to love and care for our family.

I am truly blessed to see her birthday.

She is the image of God and the very essence of me.

I love her because of God within me.

God is our reality and so it must be

That when I love her, God's love flows through me

And when I love God, she can't resist me.

. . .

God is our reality. He made us from the dust we see,

Created us to be husband and wife for eternity.

I love her because God loves me.

I am the essence of him and so is she.

I am the image of him and so it must be

That when I love her, I love me.

So Happy Birthday to you my love

From your loving family,

We celebrate your love

Because it's God's gift of love to me.

I CRIED TODAY

I cried today, I couldn't help myself.

    The tears just started coming for no reason at all.

I hadn't hurt myself or received a sad or depressing call.

I just started crying for no reason at all.

I cried today, I felt the tears run down my cheekbone.

I tried to think if there was anything wrong.

The more I searched the more I moaned.

I cried today, wiping the tears as fast as I could

But they just kept coming like a flood

All my efforts to stop were in vain

I looked like a mess, distressed an disdained

At that moment I realized I was feeling unreleased pain.

. . .

I cried today, wishing yesterday was tomorrow

And that I could relive it again.

Wishing time could turn back

And I could start over again.

Wishing I could be reborn

And come out in a new era

A new time, starting over as myself again.

I cried today, over words never spoken

And the faith that was broken

Over time never spent

And the love that was rent

Over risks that were taken

And the heart I was breaking

Over decisions I was making

And the consequences I was accepting.

I cried today, for being forgiven

But not forgiving myself

For falling for a lie

And not being true to myself

For not loving my wife and always satisfying myself.

. . .

I cried today, I felt so miserable

That life was barely livable.

The pain was quite considerable

Re-living all my mistakes was almost unbearable.

But I cried anyway, trying to make the pain go away

Trying to clear my mind of memories

That will forever stay.

I cried today and I thank God could

Because my emotions were not shut off

And my conscience was still good.

I cried for myself because I am the only one who knows

The incredible pain that I have caused in my life

The sleepless nights and the emotional tolls

I cried today, and I'll probably cry tomorrow

I'll cry until I drain all the sorrow.

The pain is buried in the deep marrow of my bones

So I'll probably keep crying until God calls me home.

ME

I see but I don't see,
      I hear but I don't hear,
I say but I don't say.
I live but I don't live,
I eat but I don't eat,
I laugh but I don't laugh,
I sleep but I don't sleep,
I rest but I don't rest.

I am always striving
For the best in me,
Accepting every
challenge and test for me,
Never thinking anything

Is too tough for me
Because I dream, you see.

Never facing the reality of me,
Choosing façades
And fallacies,
To help cope with the
Realities of me. It is like I'm me
But at the same time not me.

Always falling short of
What I ought to be.
Never finishing the plans
I have set for me,
Striving to be what I can be,
In spite of my history.
Every day I make history,
The history of me.

Now the task for me
Is to live in the present I see,
Always being cognizant
Of my family that surrounds me.

. . .

To see what I haven't seen,

To hear what I haven't heard,

To say what I haven't said,

To live like I've never lived,

To eat like I've never eaten.

To laugh like I've never laughed,

To sleep like I've never slept,

To rest like I've never rested,

To be me, nothing but me,

The real me,

The present me,

So help me,

God.

MY TIREDNESS IS TRYING TO TRICK ME

Too busy to eat, too tired to sleep

  Too busy to stop work, too tired, play hurt

Too busy to write, too tired at night

Too busy to watch TV, too tired for family

Too busy to talk, too tired to walk.

My tiredness is trying to trick me

Into thinking that I am sick when I am just busy

I get sick to my stomach nauseatingly

Pain surrounds my head completely

Twitch in my eye that drives me crazy

Blurred vision when trying to write and see.

My tiredness is trying to trick me

So that I can reduce my productivity

Rob me of quality time with my family

I need to stay busy instead of falling for this trickery

My stomach, head, and eyes need to get with me

Instead of beguiling me into thinking

I'm down for the count, you see.

I'm not sick or in pain

It's all just a mind game

No twitch in my eye that I cannot contain

No blurred vision that my glasses will not correct

Just hard work, from which no one can ever get hurt.

My tiredness is trying to trick me

Into thinking that I am sick when I am just busy.

TRYING TO SLEEP

*L*aying down

   Sitting up

Trying to Sleep

Time to get up.

5 o'clock the alarm rings

Get in the shower

And start to sing

Words to songs

I can't remember.

Ruby wakes up

From her slumber

And yells to stop singing

So early in the morning.

MY STRENGTH

*H*ow paradoxical my strength is to me

    For in my weakness, I am as strong as an be

Contrary to what others might see

God is my strength and only He.

He takes care of all my wants and endless needs

And all I have to do is follow his lead

Occasionally I forget that He is my strength indeed

And become his rival in meeting all my needs.

In my weakness God has accessibility

To show that man's extremity is his opportunity

When I am weak, then I am strong

And can do battle with the enemy who rages on

Seeking to kill me and to tear away my faith.

But God is always on time and has never been late
What can my little old strength do anyway?
To mention is almost senseless to say.

Can I create the air I breathe?
Or make the earth bear fruit on trees?
Can I stop the wind from blowing?
Or the floods from destroying?

Can I keep my heart beating throughout eternity?
Or awake from death's slumber to face reality?
I can do all things through Christ who strengthens me
He is my strength in weakness
And He will always be.

IT IS WELL

It is well with my soul
     Not because I exchange it for gold
Not because I've done everything I've been told
Not because I haven't strayed from the fold
Not because with my faith I've been bold
Not because I've carried my brother's load
Not because I stood up for Jesus and put up with the scold.

It is well with my soul because Jesus' blood
Is more precious than gold
Because I believe the gospel that I have been told
Because God exchanged his Son for my soul
He took death's debt, and paid my toll

Made me his Son and put me on this eternal roll.

It is well with my soul

And there is nothing that I can do but be bold

And tell the story of the infinite value of the soul

Praise the Lord for saving my imperfect, precious soul.

BETWEEN A HUSBAND AND WIFE

What is love between a husband and wife?
Sometimes it's as hot as fire
Sometimes it's as cold as ice.

Waxing and waning between hot and cold
One thing's for sure, it never gets old
From death do us part, the preacher man said
So in love we will be until the day we both are dead.

I know why I love you so very much
It's your smile, your eyes, and your tender touch
It fills me so much with a feeling I can't describe
If at once it all left me, I believe I would die.

. . .

So when I wake up in the morning and see you lying next to me

I thank the Lord for you and for also saving me

I'm going to do right by the wife God has given me

And have the kind of love that will last throughout eternity.

ART

Bright colors on picture frames
      That speak to me in a language that I cannot fully
understand.

People, places, and weird things

Reflections of our culture in this land.

All come from canvas or paper, pencil, pen, or brush,

And sometimes all are in the artist's plan,

Or is it a plan at all, but rather a journey that his mind

Takes his body through as a conductor leads a band.

The result is a symphony of colors and shapes,

Land and seascapes, faces and bodies, heaven and its host,

Hell and its host, cities and worlds in faraway lands.

Speak to me, you work of human expression:

Tell me your artist's confession,
Give me a picture of his soul's possession
Of thoughts, ideals, and measures of pain.

I came to marvel and to be moved
By the creative energy of the artist's soul
He speaks to my soul when his work I behold
And I am silenced,
Moved to the joy of contemplation.

CHRISTMAS

*T*he world is so awesome

When Christmas season arrives,

You would think the devil had left the earth

And gone to the underside.

People are warm and friendly

And seek out their loved ones

With family pride and fellowship

With neighbors and friends

To ensure those relationships are tied.

I love the ambience of Christmas

And how it turns moans into happy tones.

Even people who get on your nerves

Take a vacation and leave you alone.

It's a time to think about Jesus

And how our sins with His blood He did atone,

And that He was crucified on the cross

When He had done nothing wrong.

My family is blessed to know Jehovah God,

In whom we believe,

And Jesus Christ, His only Son,

Whom by faith we have wholeheartedly received.

We are blessed to have family and friends

And rejoice that they too have believed

That Jesus got up from the grave, and the weeds

He lives and meets all of our needs.

We are happy that Christmas is a day

To honor the birth of Christ

And pray that this season

Many will know that He is the way

The truth, and life.

. . .

So on Christmas day

When you open the gifts that you have received

Thank God for His gift of love

And Jesus in whom you believe.

MOTHERS

*M*others are the foundation of the family

Mothers are the backbone of the church

Mothers are the love in the world.

Mothers are the vessels of life

Mothers are the nurturers and mentors of greatness

Mothers are the hands and arms of God.

Every president

King, Queen

Prince, and Royal have a mother.

Every Congressman

Or woman, Senator

Governors, and Mayors have a mother.

Every Civil Rights leader

Community leader

Evangelist, Preacher

Elder, Deacon

And musicians have a mother.

Every mother

Father, Sister

And Brother has a mother.

Motherhood is woven into the fabric of life

Motherhood is part of our identity and spirituality

We celebrate our mothers

And our church mothers

Because of what they bring to our lives.

A love that no man can ever have

Is a mother's love

Our mother's love is all-encompassing love

That Godly love

That special love.

. . .

A love that brings peace,

When there is conflict,

A love that brings happiness,

When there is sadness.

A love that brings,

Soothing relief when there is pain,

A love that brings A good word,

when there are no words,

A love that brings Laughter,

When you really want to cry.

A love that brings,

Wisdom when there is confusion,

A love that brings,

Solutions when there are problems.

Mothers and especially Church mothers,

Are blessings from God.

They epitomize the light of the world,

And the salt of the earth,

Showing forth God's goodness,

Mercy, and grace.

. . .

Divinely appointed,

Spiritually gifted,

Powerfully anointed,

Church mothers are to be praised with high honors.

They are blessed and sanctified,

For the work that God is doing,

Through them in the church,

They bring love.

Mothers are God's Love

Personified.

I AM NOT A POET, BUT MONET
HAMILTON IS

I am not a poet,

But you are Monet.

My poems are from the cortex.

Your poems are from the vortex.

Otherworldly is your middle name

And truth is your nickname.

You speak for the living and nonliving

Things that have no voices.

You see what can only be seen

By the mind's eye.

You sense what can only be felt
By your spirit at the highest level of consciousness.

Tell me again, poet,
How the walls feel and what the smells say?

Tell me again, poet, about those who have walked the halls before
And have left holes and marks that are their signatures of life.

I am not a poet is what I say,
When I read words that jump off the page.

And into my mind and will not shut up
As they become a lyrical refrain.

And all I can do is call out the name of the poet.
And worship what they have birthed into the universe.

And declare in my soul that I am not a poet
But hold on to the dream of what I aspire to be:

. . .

A poet whose words jump off the page and into the hearts and souls

Of those who would dare to read, less they also are changed in an instant.

I am not a poet,

But you are Monet Hamilton.

MY LIFE

My life, my way, my tears, my fears, my love,
My hate, my weakness, my strength, my cool,
My hot, my anger, my calm, my glut, my want,

My worry, my confidence, my jealousy, my security,
My sadness, my happiness, my lost, my found,
My memory, my forgetfulness, my forgiveness, my grudge,

My peace, my turmoil, my joy, my despair, my happiness,
My frustration, my favorite, my enemy, my worst,
My best, my courage, my fear, my debt, my assets,

My wealth, my poverty, my benevolence, my covetousness,
My fight, my reconciliation, my payback, and my let it go,

My sickness, my health, my heart, my mind, my eyes,

My soul, my hair, my vanity, my skin, my identity,

My color, my plight, my clothes, my message,

My shoes, my statement, my feet, my hands, my toes,

My fingers, my legs, my arms, my face, my nose, my lips,

My teeth, my forehead, my wrinkles, my ears, my lobes,

My beard, my mustache, my cheeks, my butt, my *other* parts,

My mouth, my mind, my thoughts, my depression,

My exaggerations, my lies, my stories, my sermons,

My motivation, my lessons, my house, my car, my dog,

My bed, my wife, my children, my friends, my neighbors,

My pastor, my employees, my employer, my boss, my goals,

My plans, my trips, my vacations, my money, my time, my wine,

My beer, my Hennessy, my Grey Goose, my watermelon, my strawberries,

My oranges, my grits, my bacon, my eggs over easy,

My ham, my fried chicken, my corn bread, my collard greens,

My black-eyed peas, my homemade soups, my noodles, my shrimp,

My catfish, my burritos, my tacos, my deep-fried fish,

My refried beans, my cheese, my ice cream,

My oatmeal and raisin cookies, my basketball, my golf,

My racquetball, my bike, my running, my exercise, my beach,

My sand, my ocean, my pool, my putting green, my theater,

My movies, my music, my phone, my tablet, my vinyl, my CDs,

My laptop, my online radio, my people, my history, my country,

My president, my Jesus, my God, my Holy Spirit

My soul, my spirit, my eternity, my destiny,

My death.

REFLECTIONS

*P*eace

   When war and hate cease.

Joy

When love is employed.

Love

When sacrifice is demonstrated.

God

When we realize that there is no one else we can depend on.

DON'T LIE TO YOURSELF

I'm going *to* do this,
    I'm going to do that,
I'm going to lose weight,
But here I sit getting fat.
Don't lie to yourself.

I'm going to work hard,
I'm going to work smart,
I'm going to meet my commitments,
But here I am in the mall with a shopping cart.
Don't lie to yourself.

I'm going to start school,
I'm going to finish my degree,

I'm going to do all my homework,

But here I sit watching TV.

Don't lie to yourself.

I am going to be debt free

I am going to save money

I am going to create a budget

But here I am applying for more Credit Cards

Don't lie to yourself.

I am going to improve my credit

I am going to stop spending money

I am going to take a HUD homeownership class

I am going to get pre-approved for home loan

I am going to buy a home before the end of the year.

But here I am 10 years later renting and broke.

Don't lie to yourself.

Be true to yourself, and

DO it for yourself.

GOOD GROUND

Matt. 13:3-9 KJV

*S*tones, thorns, and good ground

Are all homes where the seed of faith is sown.

Stony, thorny, and good ground

Are the hearts that must be broken or plowed when found.

Lord, when I heard the gospel it shook me to my bone.

I knew I wanted God to be my father and heaven my future home.

When I heard the gospel it was like a heavy weight being lifted from me

And blinders taken off my eyes so that I could see.

My heart of stone was crushed into pieces

And I believed in a savior called Jesus.

It was like a plow that went straight through me

Pulling all the weeds away so that I could see

It was like the rain that would not stop falling

And flooded my heart and gave me a new calling.

I thank you, Father,

For drawing me and helping me to see my need for Thee.

I know now that I am good ground

Because my faith in Your Son is still pure and sound.

Thank you for breaking my heart and making me good ground.

I LOVE TO SING

I love to sing because of how God makes me feel.

Each note and word is filled with

Meaning and rhythm in every song.

It brings my mind into focus about my spiritual life,

My relationship to Christ, and how my God is real.

I love to sing because of how God makes me feel.

It takes my mind to a spiritual and emotional high.

I think about the providence of God,

The doors He has opened,

And how He has delivered me from every ordeal.

I love to sing because of how it makes me feel.

I just want to give God his props,

Offer him spiritual sacrifices,

Petitions of gratitude,

Demonstrate my dependence on him

In prayer when I kneel.

I love to sing because of how God makes me feel,

The feeling of salvation because of His sacrifice for me.

The grace I have been given because

He died on the cross for me.

His resurrection is for me.

Death is not my reality but a door to eternity.

So I thank Him for the day, and night,

And the air I breathe, for keeping my heart beating and still.

I love to sing because of how God makes me feel.

CRAZY LOVE

I love you for sentimental reasons
    And adore everything about you.
Your smile, your style, your personality,
And your intelligence makes everyone take notice.
Our love grows with every change of season
Because of the change that has taken place within us.

We laugh and cry, we fight and argue,
And we stop and do it all over again
Because we are two different people who love each other.

I love you more today than I ever have.
You make our home our life and you are my wife.
As a woman you have made me a man.

As my wife you have made me a husband

And a father of four children.

Your scent, your softness,

Your warmth captivates my mind.

I think about you all the time.

I love you because I can't help myself.

I love you more than life itself.

I need you and cannot live life without you.

You make me crazy.

And I love you more each day.

I AM THINKING ABOUT ME!

I ain't thinking about you,

  And all the things you do.

All you do is do you.

Your first, and middle name is you,

and your last name is I.

I want this and I want that,

Never do you consider me in all of that,

Me is your nickname and I is your last name,

What have you done for me lately,

Is your daily mantra and it's driving me insane?

I ain't thinking about you.

Because you never think about me

Are you aware of all the things I do?

To make you you! Yes, I make you you.

Look at you. That is my work.

You didn't get here on your own.

Your look is because of me.

Your education would not have happened without me.

Your job couldn't be possible without me.

Your life would not be what it is without me.

I gave birth to our children and raised them up.

I feed you and the family and nourish your bodies.

I got up in the middle of the night to take care of the kids so you could go to work.

I went to the parent teachers conferences.

Helped the kids with their homework.

Took them to sport practices,

And took care of them when they were hurt.

I am your eye candy at your job functions.

I am your lover, caretaker, chef and homemaker.

I am your motivator.

I am your truth teller.

I am your healer.

I am your protector.

I am your decorator.

I am your stylist.

I am your maid.

I am the one covering you.

I am the one that cleans up after you.

I am the one who deals with all of your shit.

Especially when your shit splatters on me.

Who are you?

What are you?

Can I even count on you?

Always thinking about yourself.,

And never thinking about me.

I ain't thinking about you no more.

I am thinking about me.

So I am going to do me.

It's my time to shine!

It's my time to be served!

It's my time to have power!

It's my time to go to school!

It's my time to travel!

It's my time to take time for myself!

It's my time to see what I can do.

It's my time to live on my own terms.

When not everything is all about you,

And can now be about me.

I ain't thinking about you anymore honey

I am thinking about me.

HOW SHOULD I FEEL?

When I wake up in the morning, I know I cannot trust my feelings for several reasons.

I did not sleep well. Or I had a nightmare, or I was reliving the yesterday and second guessing my decisions or my actions.

I made a mistake, or I lost a deal or disappointed a friend or family member.

There are a thousand reasons why I cannot trust my feelings.

The number one reason I cannot trust my feelings is that my feelings rarely represent the truth about what is really going on in my life.

My feelings lie but my eyes tell the truth.

I can't trust what I feel but I can trust what I see.

Let me say that again. I can't trust what I feel but I can trust what I see.

. . .

You see - I see. I am not in darkness nor have I moved into the light of immortality. I see.

I see clearly and I am here. I can see the breath coming from my body.

I can hear the beat of my heart and feel and taste the water I drink and the food I eat.

I am alive, moving, and singing and crying and laughing and setting my agenda for a new day.

I am not sure how I feel but despite my uncertainty about my feelings, I am here.

I am here with my wife and my beautiful children and grandchildren

I am here in a beautiful home. My shelter, my fortress, my estate.

I am here living, loving, working, making money, providing for my family.

I am here with my business partners, associates, and employees who help me be me.

I am here with my friends and extended family who support me to be me.

I am here. I am alive and I am full of gratitude because I am not alone.

I am not alone. God woke me from my slumber last night and so I am here.

I am not alone. God gave me my mind today so I can reflect and remember and think and so I am here.

I am not alone. God kept my heart beating through the night and maintained the strength in my body and so I am here. Standing on my own power.

I am not alone. God enabled me to move and live and to engage with creation and beautiful people in my life and so I am here.

I am not alone. I am loved. I am protected. I am divinely equipped with skills and abilities. I am empowered. I can see, hear, speak, move, and do anything I put my mind to do. I am here.

So tell me how should I feel?

CHANGE

Change is the most constant and recurring phenomenon we will face in our lives. It is frequent, never-ending, unforgiving, unbending, untimely, and we are rarely prepared for it. It just happens.

Change can come in the middle of the night or in the middle of the day. It has no particular day of week or time of the day. Any day, at any time, and any moment will do. It just happens.

Change does not consider what is going on in our life. It does not matter If you are doing well or doing poorly. It doesn't matter if you are in good health or bad health. It doesn't care if you are busy or doing nothing at all. It just happens.

Change has no respect for people. It does not care about your gender, race, color, or sexual orientation. It doesn't care if you are married or single. If you have children or no children. If you are rich or poor, working or unemployed. It just happens.

. . .

Change is coming for you, so get ready because Change does represent the status quo, or it would not be called Change. Now would it?

Change must be embraced, loved, anticipated, and enjoyed because of the new challenge it represents.

You want Change to be the status quo?

Change represents daily opportunities that the universe brings to you that are always changing, and with Change comes Fear and Hope. You choose.

If you choose to be Fearful because you may not be able to handle the Change that Change brings, then change is going to eat you alive from the inside out. You will lose confidence, cower, and shrink back in the face of Change and lose Faith and give up.

If you choose to be Hopeful because you embrace Change and are allowing it to empower you to keep pushing even harder than you did before Change showed up. You will succeed, and your Faith will propel you to even greater things.

What Fear and Hope have in common is Faith. Fear lacks Faith. Hope represents an abundance of Faith.

Change is the activator.

Change is the catalyst.

Change is the common denominator of Fear and Hope and forces us to deal with Change and to see Change one way: with Fear or Hope.

Change is woven into the fabric of our lives and cannot be avoided. It is like the weather, or darkness or sunlight.

Change is the air we breathe.

We cannot escape Change except through death, and many choose death instead of Change. Fear and Hope are immutable participants in our lives and remind us of the ever-present reality of Change.

Embrace Change because Change has embraced you.

DID YOU ENJOY THIS BOOK?

I sure hope so!

Please join our family and write a review. Reviews are the "tip jar" of the book publishing industry. New readers weigh reviews heavily in deciding to make a purchase. You being so generous as to share your experience is the lifeblood of the success of "The Power Poetry Collection".

I appreciate you!
Eric Lawrence Frazier

SCAN ME

ERIC LAWRENCE FRAZIER, MBA BUSINESS BOOKS

THE POWER IS NOW MEDIA

The Power Is Now Media is an online multimedia company founded in 2009 by Eric L. Frazier MBA, headquartered in Riverside, California. We are advocates for homeownership, wealth building, and financial literacy. We create and publish original educational content about real estate through nationally syndicated Radio, Podcasts, Magazines, TV, Social Media, Streaming platforms, and special online seminars and webinars. We are an online platform and resource for everyone to learn about homeownership, housing, loan programs, and down payment assistance to achieve financial literacy and the American dream of homeownership. We are supported by housing finance agencies, real estate associations, and civic, religious, and community organizations. We help them amplify their voice about the services and programs they offer in lending, housing, and homeownership. Visit us at www.thepowerisnow.com

The Mission of the Power is Now Media is to inspire and educate consumers and real estate professionals to build wealth through the acquisition, management, and sale of real estate with information and support we provide via our website, live and on-demand TV, and social media platforms that empower everyone to own real estate now and achieve the American dream of homeownership. Our company slogan is "We are leading the conversation about real homeownership."

The Power Is Now Media corporate office is located at 3739 6th Street, Riverside, CA 92501. Telephone/Fax: 800-401-8994. Eric Lawrence Frazier MBA is a California Licensed Loan Originator (NMLS License #461807) and Real Estate Broker (License #O1148434).

ABOUT THE AUTHOR

Mr. Eric Lawrence Frazier MBA is the President, and CEO of The Power Is Now Media, The Power Is Now is a multimedia company that specializes in real estate education for consumers and real estate professionals on various topics in real estate, lending, economics, and government policy. The information is published on The Power Is Now Media website (www.thepowerisnow.com), national online radio and podcast platforms nationwide, Major social media channels, and live-stream TV platforms.

Mr. Frazier is also the publisher and editor-in-chief of The Power Is Now Magazines, which are online real estate magazines first published on September 1, 2013. These magazines focus on real estate education, real estate homes for sale, and national real estate news. Mr. Frazier is a graduate of Redlands University in Redlands, California, and has an MBA with an emphasis in finance and a BS in business administration and management. He has lectured at the University of California Riverside on the US mortgage crisis to international business leaders from India and has served as an adjunct professor.

With nearly four decades of originations, management, underwriting, operations, and marketing experience, Mr. Frazier is nationally known as a mortgage lending professional. He has over thirty years of experience in real estate sales as a licensed California real estate agent and over twenty years of experience as a real estate broker (#01143484).

He and his wife are the founders of Frazier Group Reality. (fraziergrouprealty.com), a-full-service,family-owned-and-operated real estate company in Riverside, California. Mr. Frazier is the former president of the Orange County Realtist, which was a chapter of the National Association of Real Estate Brokers (NAREB), and former director of the California Association of Real Estate Brokers. He is a former vice president of the Orange County National Association of Hispanic Real Estate Professionals and a former advisory board member of the Orange County Asian Real Estate Association of America.

He is also on the board of directors of the Riverside Fair Housing Council; the board of directors of Project Tomorrow (tomorrow.org), a national education nonprofit; a member of the 100 Black Men of America and the NAACP; a pastor; and leader of The Power Is Now Ministries. He is a member of the National Association of Mortgage Brokers, the Pacific West Realtors Association of Realtors, the California Association of Realtors (CAR), and the National Association of Realtors (NAR). He is the past president and director of the State of California African American Museum (www.caamuseum.org) and a former pastor of the North Fontana Church.

Mr. Frazier is also an author, singer, poet, and songwriter. He is a blogger, motivational speaker, business consultant, business coach for profit and non profit companies, and community leader. He enjoys golf, running, and jazz music. Mr. Frazier strives to be a role model for African American men and enjoys mentoring and coaching young people and adults. His greatest accomplishments are being married to the love of his life for over forty years and being the father of four daughters. His three oldest daughters have master's degrees in management and business, and his youngest daughter has a bachelor's degree in apparel merchandising and management. All of Mr. Frazier's accomplishments and associations can be found at www.linkedin.com/in/ericfrazier.

FOLLOW ME ON SOCIAL MEDIA

Lets Connect

LET'S CONNECT ON LINKEDIN